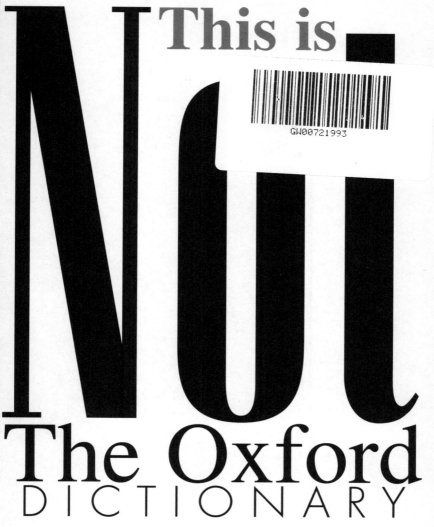

This is

Not

The Oxford

DICTIONARY

An Amusing Language Database

Compiled by Joel Rothman

Published in the UK by
POWERFRESH Limited
21 Rothersthorpe Crescent
Northampton
NN4 8JD

Telephone   0845 130 4565
Facsimile   0845 130 4563
E Mail info@powerfresh.co.uk

Copyright © 2002
Cover and interior layout by Powerfresh
Cover Illustration Sanjit Saha

ISBN   1904967000

Printed in Malta by Gutenberg Press Ltd
Powerfresh September 2004

For all those people who bother to look up the meaning of words and expressions.

Atom Bomb:
An explosive device under which all men are cremated equal.

Supersonic Jet Fighter:
A great plane — it allows you to retreat at over 1000 miles per hour.

Syrian General:
A man who's treated for delusions of grandeur — he thinks he's an Israeli private.

Nigerian Navy:
A great service — there's none of this nonsense about women and children first.

Army Cook:
A man who, when he's discharged can't get a job. After all, every recipe he knows ends with, "Serves 2000."

Young Women:
Females who don't like their rice steamed or fried — they prefer it thrown.

Puffed Rice:
What you throw at weddings when the bride is expecting.

Dove of Peace:
A bird that's a little cuckoo these days.

Female University Graduate:
A young woman who complains, "Four years of college and who has it got me?"

Wedding Ring:
A one-man band. Like a tourniquet it stops your circulation.

Fairy Tale Ending:
... and so they lived happily even after.

Forty:
A time when life begins — to show.

Middle Age:
Halfway between adolescence and obsolescence.

Time:
A great healer — but it doesn't do much for beauty.

Ageing Woman:
A female who is so concerned about growing old that overnight she turned blonde with worry.

Cosmetics:
A woman's way of keeping a man from reading between the lines.

Old Age:
A time when parents discover that stockings support and children don't.

Therapy:
When you pay 100 pounds an hour to look at the ceiling and squeal on yourself.

Therapist:
Someone who encourages you to speak freely, then charges a fortune for listening.

Psychiatrist:
A person who'll listen to you as long as you don't make sense.

Neurotic:
A low-budget psychotic.

Auto Mechanic:
A man who, if he goes to a psychiatrist, is told to get under the couch.

Eyelids:
Windshield wipers for contact lenses.

Nose:
A snot machine, and another thing that should be seen and not heard.

Anatomy:
Something we all have, but looks much better on women.

Masseurs:
People who knead people.

Political Jokes:
Not so funny— too often they get elected.

True Desperation:
An obese woman shaving her head before weighing herself on the bathroom scale.

True Optimist:
A karate expert walking up to a Sequoia tree.

Politics:
The second oldest profession, but it bears an uncanny resemblance to the first.

Politicians:
Like diapers they should be changed often, and for the same reason.

Politician's Speech:
A public oration in which you hear loads of facts you could never find anywhere else.

Political Left:
So-called because it's so far from right.

Liberal:
Someone with both feet planted firmly in the air.

Conservatism:
A step in the right direction.

Conservatives:
Politicians who work for a better yesterday. They believe in continually moving forward in the direction of the status quo.

Communism:
A social / economic system of government where it's dog eat dog, as opposed to capitalism which is the opposite.

Russian Citizen:
A man who spits and his friend says, "Igor—let's not talk politics."

Feudalism:
A time when it was your count that votes.

Upright Piano:
An instrument that can be downright annoying.

Thoughtful Child:
A kid who, when his hands are filthy, will practice piano using only the black notes.

Harmonica Players:
Experts at eating corn-on-the-cob.

Double Bass:
The only instrument for which, you first have to pass a height requirement.

Bagpipe Player:
One who could easily get a job on a farm milking cows.

Xylophone:
An instrument for converting timber into timbre.

Beginning Violinist:
Someone who has to start from scratch.

Jasha Heifitz:
A man who was always up to his chin in music.

Crazy Violinists:
They'll actually pay more for an instrument that's hundreds of years old than they will for one that is brand new.

Harp:
A nude piano.

Harpists:
Musicians who, when they retire, no longer give a pluck.

Heaven:
A place that's overmanned in the string section.

Beehive:
A sting ensemble.

Secretary:
A woman who tells her date, "Stop and/or I'll slap your face."

Diplomacy:
The art of being able to explain your wife to your secretary.

Chutspah:
A secretary asking for an extra days vacation to make up for all the coffee breaks she missed while on vacation.

Lateness:
A good thing — it helps to cut down on the number of mistakes you make during the day.

Cad:
An artist who invites a woman to see his etchings, then tries to sell her one.

Avant-garde Artist:
Someone who throws paint at a canvas, wipes the paint with a cloth, then sells the cloth for a small fortune.

Dali's Mother:
The Mama of Dada.

Modern Painting:
Something you purchase to cover up a crack in your wall. A short time later you decide the crack looks much better.

Vincent van Gogh:
A man whose famous last words were, "Speak up!"

Eve:
The first woman who said, "I have nothing to wear," and meant it.

Adam:
Eve's mother.

Astronauts Wife:
The only happily married woman who can truly say, "My husband is just out of this world."

Ludicrous:
Two astronauts arguing over which one will get the seat next to the window.

Space Program:
Made medical history—it was the first time a capsule ever took a man.

Mars:
The suburbs of Earth.

Dog:
Man's best friend because it wags its tail instead of its tongue.

Unlucky Husband:
A guy who owns three dogs but the only one that barks at him is his wife.

Christopher Columbus:
An explorer who was at sea for many months. When he finally spotted land with trees on the horizon he became ecstatic — and so did his dog.

Pavlov:
A name that rings a bell.

Dog Sled:
A polar coaster.

Dog Catcher:
A man with a seeing dog eye.

Bitch:
The one responsible for teaching her pups about the birds and the fleas.

Great Dane Puppy:
A dog that has the house broken before it's housebroken.

Chihuahua:
A bonsai Great Dane.

Pit Bull Puppy:
A young dog who will, in no time, be eating out of your ankle.

Rottweiler:
You get it as a puppy, feed it, walk it, train it, play with it, take it to the vet when it's sick, give it all the love and affection you've got, and ten years later — it tries to rip out your throat.

Bald Man:
The first to know when it rains.

Delusion:
A bald man refusing to believe he's lost that much hair, claiming he simply has a wide part.

Bald Optimist:
A man without hair going into a pharmacy buying a bottle of hair restorer along with an expensive hair brush.

Toupee:
Ear-to-ear carpeting.

Hippie:
A guy who walks into a barbershop and says, "Take a little off the hips."

Gossip:
Someone who syndicates their conversation. They have a lot of friends —to speak of.

Ann Boleyn:
A woman who talked her head off.

Deaf Blabbermouth:
One who is such a talker that other deaf people can't get a finger in edgewise.

Big Ben:
The tock of the town.

Hypochondriac:
Someone who, after being told they're in perfect health, insists upon a second opinion.

Radiation:
Absolutely nothing to worry about —after all, it contains no cholesterol.

Basketball:
A sport in which any boy can be a star when he grows up, up, up.

Football:
The one sport which, for many people, is a matter of life and death. For others it's much more important than that.

Good sport:
Someone who has to lose to prove it. He or she grips the winners hand even though they'd prefer it to be the throat!

Fishing:
A jerk at one end of a rod waiting for a jerk at the other end.

Amateur Athlete:
Someone who's paid only in cash.

Vacations:
The boss tells you when, and your wife tells you where.

Passport Photo:
Look at it and you'll be convinced you're too sick to travel.

College Education:
What enables you to get a high-paying job in a company often owned by a school dropout.

Anatomy Professor:
A man who tells a woman, "I love you with all my heart, liver, kidneys and soul."

Incompetent Nurse:
One who's been reprimanded because she was told to prick his boil, not. . .

Tension:
What the sergeant shouts to his troops.

Macaroni:
The man who first invented radio.

Conservation:
When you talk to people.

Magnets:
Those little creatures you find in rotten apples.

Zinc:
What you do when you can't swim.

Duck:
A chicken in snowshoes.

Bread:
Raw toast.

Raisin:
A worried grape.

Singing:
Every man's bathright.

Crooner:
A man with his heart in his throat.

Folk Singer:
Someone who sings about the joys of the simple life with a £10,000 sound system.

Country Music:
Pop corn. It's often sung by ear through the nose.

Terrible Singer:
A man who sounds so bad that deaf people even refuse to watch his lips move.

Rock Music:
A loud beat with blaring guitars, convincing some people that the world won't end with only a bang but also with a twang.

Rock Musicians:
The players are only aware of three dynamic levels —loud, louder, and deafening.

Punk Rock:
Audible grime —a pain in the ear, and the highest form of noise.

Music Manager:
A guy who gets aggravated at the thought that some bum rock group can command 85 - 90% of his salary.

Teenage Atheist:
A kid who doesn't believe in Elvis Presley.

Expert Archer:
A person who is so accurate he can, with his bow and arrow, circumcise a male housefly in midflight at 100 yards.

Jewish Juggler:
Someone who can feel guilty about six different things at the same time.

Practical Joker Husband:
A man who buys his wife 50 hats, then puts her in a room without a mirror.

Practical Joker Father:
A guy who takes his kids to the beach and buries them in the sand up to their waste —head first!

Union Official:
A man who tells his kid a bedtime story and begins, "Once upon a time-and-a-half. . ."

Whisky Producers:
People who pay their workers time-and-a-fifth.

U.K. Mint Workers:
The only people who go on strike to make less money.

Picketing:
A time that tries men's soles.

Government Workers:
People who vote for a go-slow strike and nobody notices the difference.

Money:
Known as the root of all evil, but it's not true —it's the lack of it. They say that money talks, but for most people it only says, "Goodbye."

I.O.U:
A paper wait.

Misers:
Strange people who are always willing to live within their means. They firmly believe a friend in need is a friend you don't need.

Philanthropist:
A wealthy person who gives away what he should be giving back.

Poverty:
It's when someone asks, "Do you have money in the bank?" and you answer, "I'm not sure —let me shake it."

Wealth:
A curse — especially when your neighbours have it.

Rabbit Circumcision:
A Hare cut.

Luxurious House:
Where the hot and cold running water is Perrier.

Filthy Rich:
A woman pushing a shopping cart through Tiffanys.

Credit Card Holders:
Members of the debt set.

Plastic Surgery:
Cutting up your wife's credit cards.

True Snob:
A passenger who takes a cruise, but declines an invitation to dine at the captain's table, refusing to eat with the help.

Pollution:
Grime in the streets.

Air Pollution:
Mother Nature making us pay through the nose.

Los Angeles:
A city where you get airsick after you get off a plane. When the fog finally lifts you can see the smog. In the morning you open the windows and listen to the birds coughing.

Bore:
Someone with nothing to say and says it.

Bad Smog:
When you think you see a Blue Jay but it's only a Cardinal holding its breath.

Noise Pollution:
A relative thing. In a city it's a jet plane taking off — in a monastery it's a pen that scratches.

Smoking:
Something that kills live men but cures dead swine.

Light Smokers:
People who are proud of themselves for being able to get through just one lighter per day.

Smoker's Cough:
Not all bad— for some people it's the only exercise they get.

Bad Air:
When firemen are treated for smoke inhalation and it's their day off.

Positive Thinker:
A man who comes home and discovers cigar butts under the bed, so he assumes his wife has given up smoking cigarettes.

Restaurant:
Where the food that is served has often been frozen — it's the staff that's fresh.

Exclusive Restaurant:
If you order Perrier the waiter asks, "What year?"

Open Air Restaurant:
When there's heavy rain it could take three hours to finish your soup.

Cairo:
A city with great restaurants —millions of flies can't be wrong.

Fast Short Order Cook:
Someone who can cook minute rice in fifty seconds.

Michelin Bomb:
A "smart bomb" that destroys restaurants under two stars.

Vietnam:
A country in which the best-selling book is entitled, HOW TO WOK YOUR DOG.

Vietnamese Restaurant:
Where your waiter asks, "Would you like your main course depawed?"

Europeans:
People who are very fond of animals —especially roasted with two vegetables.

Vegetarian:
A person who won't eat anything that has a mother.

Vegetarian Restaurant:
Where every main dish is a vegetable —served with two vegetables.

Bribe:
A sort of gift. The giver says, "Thanks," the receiver says, "Don't mention it."

Criminals:
People who say, "Take the money and run." (Politicians say the opposite.)

Mobster's Son:
One who wants to follow in his father's fingerprints.

Israel:
A country in which organised crime is known as the Kosher Nostra.

Jack The Ripper's Mother:
A woman who asked her son, "How come you never go out with the same woman more than once?"

Honesty:
For the most part it's less profitable than dishonesty.

Good Timing:
Dying penniless.

Smugglers:
People who do not respect the customs of their country —they have no sense of duty.

Ambitious Smuggler:
One who studies hard to better himself and finally becomes an embezzler.

Paranoid Mugger:
A thief who says, "Hand over your money or I'll kill myself!"

Kleptomaniacs:
People with the gift of grab.

Counterfeiter:
His problem is not how to make money —it's how to spend it.

Inland Revenue:
The government department that lives for bread alone.

Tax Inspector:
Another guy who knows that Britain is a land of untold wealth.

Tax Code:
The only code that breaks people.

Dachshund:
A Great Dane after taxes.

Good Accountant:
A professional who can save you lots of time — sometimes five to ten years.

Tenacious Lawyer:
One who refuses to give up. If his client is sentenced to be hanged he promises to sue for whiplash.

Life:
You can't do much about the length but you sure can do something about the width.

Reducing Expert:
Someone who lives off the fat of the land.

Wall Street Reducing Salon:
A place that's just for stocky brokers.

Dieting Cannibal:
A man who eats only pygmies.

Can't Fail Diet:
Only eat when the news is good.

Bilingual Illiterate:
Someone who can't read or write in two different languages.

Lover Of Mystery Books:
A person who reads the final chapter first. He knows who did it, but he doesn't know what they did.

Well-Read:
What you're considered if you read a lot of books. (If you watch a lot of TV are you considered well-viewed?)

Fast Speed Reader:
One who takes the day off to read the complete works of Dickens, then has nothing to do for the rest of the evening.

Racial Prejudice:
Just a pigment of one's imagination.

Africa:
A continent that produces many great runners. They have a unique training program — it's called a lion.

African Safari:
Like a reverse smorgasbord — you pay £20,000 for all that can eat you.

Cannibal:
A guy who goes into a restaurant and orders the waiter.

Cannibal Detective:
Someone who enjoys grilling his suspects.

Nairobi Airlines:
They feed the passengers in first class with the people from economy class.

G-Spot:
So called because inexperienced young men say, "Gee —where the hell is it?"

Kiss:
A strange thing —children get it for nothing, young men have to steal it, and old men have to pay for it.

Womaniser:
Just a layman, after all.

Confucius:
A wise man who once said, "Seven days on honeymoon make one hole week."

Woman with braces:
A pecker wrecker.

Kamakazi Pilot:
A guy who has to do all his bragging ahead of time.

Experience:
What you have long after you've forgotten her name.

48-38-48:
The measurements of a truly buxom woman. The other breast is usually a bit smaller.

Whore:
The kind of woman who wants more out of sex than just pleasure.

Sick Hooker:
A woman who is told to stay off her back 'til she feels better.

Great Swimmer:
A street walker in Venice.

Mermaid:
A pinup tadpole.

Nudist Colony:
Where you discover that all men are not created equal.

Microwave Bed:
A new invention — you get eight hours sleep in three minutes.

Perfect Pair:
The husband's a pill his wife's a headache.

Honest Washing Machine:
One with four settings: RINSE, FADE, SHRINK, TEAR.

Loud Alarm Clock:
A device designed to scare the daylights into you.

Fluoridated Socks:
The latest in soft footwear —you never get a hole in them.

Bad Idea:
Putting someone who stutters in charge of the xerox machines.

TV:
Bubble gum for the eyes.

Major Mistake:
Starting up a new business in a fireproof building.

Recipe For Success:
About the same as that for a nervous breakdown.

Smart Boss:
One who makes sure he doesn't get ulcers —he gives them.

Compassionate Boss:
A person who never says, "You're fired!" Instead, he gently says, "You're dehired."

Civic-Minded Boss:
One who does his part to save energy—in winter he doesn't heat the office.

Inflation:
Being broke with loads of money in your pocket.

Cost Of Living:
The difference between your net income and your gross habits.

Rents:
They're now so high that for the first time in history leases are breaking people.

Thrift:
A great virtue — especially in your ancestors.

True Spendthrift:
Someone who overdraws on an unlimited expense account.

Budget:
A systematic way of living beyond your means.

Today's Movies:
Not only larger than life —they're dirtier.

Porn Flick:
A dirty film in which a star always emerges.

X-Rated Movie:
One with an underdeveloped plot —but the cast isn't.

Good Old Days:
A time when actors played parts —today they reveal them.

Unhappy Porn Actress:
One who doesn't like the parts she's given to play with.

Hollywood Starlet:
A woman who complains, "Always the bride, never the bridesmaid."

Washington D.C. Resident:
If it's an attractive woman, she's often the object of a long congressional probe.

Unlucky Girlfriend:
One whose boyfriend doesn't drink, smoke, or take drugs. But what he does do is make his own dresses.

Sick Transexual:
A woman who doesn't feel like himself.

Miniskirt:
A garment worn by a female that insures good male manners. Did you ever see a guy get on a bus in front of one?

Common Lie:
It's nothing but a cold sore.

Eskimo Flasher:
A man who's always in danger of developing an unusual case of frostbite.

D.O.M:
An unlucky older guy. Caught up in the sexual revolution, he's someone who's run out of ammunition.

Paedophile:
Simply child's play.

Homosexual:
A man who agrees with W.C. Fields when he said, "There's a sucker born every day."

Proctology:
A medical discipline in which you start at the bottom and stay there.

Proctologist:
Someone who believes in treating the hole person.

September:
The month when millions of bright happy faces turn toward school — they belong to the mothers.

Spring:
The time when Mama Bear says to Papa Bear, "Wake up —it's half past April."

Summer:
When we see the return of the prodigal sun.

Autumn:
When Mother Nature goes through a change of leaf.

Winter:
A 90 day cooling off period.

Wind:
Air in a hurry.

Rain:
What makes flowers emerge and taxis disappear.

Gardening:
Man's effort to improve his lot.

Gardener:
A person with a sense of humus.

Organic Gardeners:
People who till it like it is.

Amateur Gardener:
A person who's sometimes the victim of vicious plots.

Gentleman Gardener:
Someone who tips his hat every time he passes a tomato.

Grass:
Something that grows by inches but dies by feet.

Undertaker:
A man who signs his letters, "Eventually yours."

Rich Undertaker:
Someone who drives a sports hearse.

Pathologist:
When he dates a woman she can be sure he's after her body.

Suicide:
The sincerest form of self criticism.

Civil Servant:
A person who, before he takes his own life, will leave a suicide note in triplicate.

Guillotine:
A machine designed to make a man die like a salami.

Egotist:
Someone who wants to die in his own arms.

Funeral Costs:
Now so high it's easy to understand why the dead are referred to as the Dear Departed.

No Sense Advert:
COFFINS WITH A LIFETIME GUARANTEE

Widows:
There are two kinds—bereaved and relieved.

Black Garters:
Worn by some widows in memory of those who have passed beyond.

Band:
An orchestra without guts.

Perfectionist:
A musician who completes things from A to G.

Mediocre Musician:
Someone who is always at his best.

Child Prodigy:
A young kid with highly imaginative parents.

Choreographer:
Someone who uses his head to give employment to other people's feet.

Russian:
A man who sits on nothing and dances.

Limbo Dancers:
Under achievers.

Musical Plagiarist:
A composer who gives birth to an adopted child.

Songwriters:
People who are often better at remembering than at composing.

Classical Music:
To a teenager it's any music without an electric guitar.

J.S. Bach:
A great composer who would never lend money—he always claimed he was baroque.

Opera:
A wonderful form of entertainment —if it wasn't for all that singing.

Soap Opera:
Corn on the sob.

Giant Conference Table:
One that's twenty feet long, eight feet wide, and sleeps thirty.

Candle Factory:
A building where, if a fire starts, it will take over 100 firemen all day to blow out the blaze.

Confidence:
The feeling you sometimes have before you fully understand the situation.

Stockbroker:
Men who go to work by bus and train, then give financial advice to people who drive to their office in a Mercedes.

Executive:
An ulcer with authority.

Modern Flight:
So fast you can now have lunch in London then heartburn in New York.

Air India:
An airline with a unique way of feeding people. They give the passengers in economy class an empty bowl and let them beg from the first class passengers.

First Class:
A way of flying that enables you to meet a better class of hijackers.

Spiritualist:
A trance - guesser.

Air Atalia:
Their planes are easy to recognise from the hair under their wings.

Millionaire:
A guy who carries so much cash that when he flies his wallet is considered carry-on luggage.

Birth Control Pills:
Tax deductible —but only if they don't work.

Condoms:
Rubbers that are guaranteed. But if they break the guarantee runs out.

Maternity Ward:
The stork market.

Toilet Training:
Always a matter of pot luck.

Only Child:
A kid that easily gets exhausted playing on a seesaw by himself.

Childhood:
The time between hopscotch and real Scotch.

Adolescents:
Youngsters who work their fingers to the phone.

Teenagers:
Rhinestones in the rough, they're always ready to give you the benefit of their inexperience. They dress alike, eat alike, talk alike, think alike, look alike, and what are they against? Conformity!

Skinheads:
Teenagers with more hair than brains.

Teenage Hypochondriac:
One who has to be constantly reassured that there's no such thing as terminal acne.

Growing Up:
That slow painful transition from praying your face will clear to praying your check will clear.

Women:
According to men they're imperfect creatures, but the best other sex we have.

Terrible Memory:
A woman who doesn't forget a thing you tell her.

Ugly Women:
Females who are not photogenic —in person.

Female Linguists:
Women who can aggravate you in any one of five different languages.

A Woman's Place:
It's said to be in the home —and she should go there directly after work.

Stockings:
Strange leg garments —they run while women walk.

Divorce:
The future tense of marriage.

Nudist Wedding:
A festive occasion where it's easy to recognise the best man.

Sleepy Bride:
A newly married woman who's so exhausted she can't stay awake for a second.

Woman With Ten Kids:
A female who sues for divorce on the grounds of compatibility.

Alimony:
According to some husbands it's like feeding hay to a dead horse.

Gambling:
An easy way of getting nothing for something.

Racetrack:
Where windows clean people.

Pessimist:
An optimist on his way home from Vegas.

Las Vegas:
Where you'll get odds that you'll never get even.

Gambler's Child:
A kid who, by the age of three, can count from one all the way to king.

Truly Religious Man:
A guy who holds four aces and still he prays to God.

Mother Superior:
A woman who labels her files, SACRED and TOP SACRED.

Moses:
A man who said to God, "Let me make sure I understand — the Arabs get the oil and we get to cut off the tips of our WHAT?"

Taliban:
An extremist group of religious fanatics whose great fear is that someone, somewhere, somehow is having a good time.

Noah:
A biblical figure whose famous last words were, "There's nothing to worry about — it's only gonna be a light shower."

Donkey With 150 IQ:
A smart ass.

Shepherd:
A person that all kids flock to.

Favourite Animal:
For some people it's a rack of lamb.

Aardvark:
Aan aanimal like aan aanteater.

Cat:
The one animal that never cries over spilt milk.

Porcupine:
The only animal that undergoes acupuncture.

Bird Watcher:
Someone who listens to the birds with binoculars.

King Kong's Last Words:
"If you'll excuse me I have to catch a plane."

Sex:
Like a table - four bare legs and no drawers.

Octopus:
A sea creature that gets married and walks down the aisle arm in arm in arm in arm in ...

Confused Octopus:
Just a crazy mixed-up squid.

Philosophical Skunk:
An animal who contemplates the reality of its existence then concludes, "I stink, therefore I am."

Potato:
An Irish avocado.

Indecisive Insect:
A centipede whose been asked to put its best foot forward.

Mink:
An animal that exists for one reason only — to fit well.

Great Salesman:
A guy who is able to convince his wife that polyester is the generic name for mink.

Artichoke:
A loose leaf vegetable.

Alaska:
A state where they grow frozen vegetables.

Pimp:
An Australian with five sheep.

Watermelon:
A great fruit—you eat, you drink, you wash your face.

Oyster:
A fish that's built like a nut.

Cashew:
A nut with back trouble.

Fish Market:
A place that sells sole food.

Strawberry Shortcake:
So called because it's always so short on strawberries.

Cookbook:
A volume with stirring passages.

Italian Chef:
A man who is best judged by his pasta performances.

Stuffed Pepper:
A hamburger with a girdle.

Skillet:
A frying pan that's made it into high society.

Coffee:
The morning transfusion.

Toast:
A strange food —it's eaten in the morning and drunk at night.

Dairymaid:
A girl who ought to know butter.

Butcher:
A swindler on a small scale.

Lamb:
It's sheep at any price, whereas venison is always deer.

Lamb Stew:
Much ado about mutton.

Feast:
An eat wave.

Alphabet Soup:
Loose talk with vegetables.

Yeast:
To a baker it's the major source of inflation.

Mealtime:
When children sit down to continue eating.

Organic Food Restaurant:
An eating establishment where nothing is added to the food, but 30% is added to the price.

Waiter:
A guy who thinks that money grows on trays.

Independent Waiter:
He won't take orders from anyone.

Home:
Is where the heartburn is.

Etiquette:
Knowing which fingers to put in your mouth when you whistle for the waiter.

Modern Housewife:
A woman who dresses to kill, and often cooks the same way.

Modern Husband:
A man who wears the pants in the family—he also washes and irons them.

Chauvinist:
You cook, we eat.

Buffet Dinner:
Usually given when the host doesn't have enough chairs for everyone.

Marquis de Sade:
A man who never invited anyone over for a formal meal—it seems his friends just dropped in for smacks.

Film Hero:
In some films it's the person who sits through it.

X-Rate Film:
One in which the director, instead of saying "cut", says, "Pour cold water on them."

Jewish Porno Flick:
For every minute of sex there's five minute, of guilt.

Modern Film Score:
Music that's perfectly intertwined with the violence —you come out whistling the machine guns.

Avante-Garde Directors:
People who develop the most unusual scripts such as having the man and woman actually married.

Wide Screen:
A development which has made bad films seem twice as bad.

Sceptic:
A guy who sees a dozen people waiting for an elevator, but still feels compelled to push the button.

Truly Nervous Woman:
Someone who shakes so badly she can thread the needle on a sewing machine going at full speed.

Senile Grandmother:
An older woman who takes the Pill so as not to have any more grandchildren.

Specialist In Geriatrics:
A doctor who's a spreader of old wive's tails.

Thirty-Five:
The ideal age for a woman —especially if she's fifty.

Woman's Face:
What wears off as the evening wears on.

Female Loser:
A woman who's so ugly that her vibrator refuses to vibrate.

Blind Date:
Often you expect a vision and she turns out to be a sight.

Shrew:
One who throws hisses instead of kisses.

Feminist:
A woman who'd rather bring home the bacon than fry it.

Topless Ventriloquist:
A woman who's certain the audience will never notice her lips move.

Porcupine:
The only animal that regularly goes for acupuncture.

Beavers:
Animals that have a dam good time.

Miser Skunk:
One that refuses to part with a scent.

Tortoise:
One with turtle recall.

Newborn Termites:
Babes in the woods.

Irish Siamese Twins:
Two people not joined.

Idiot:
A guy who's stuck on the escalator because of a power failure.

Moron:
Someone who proof-reads the xerox copy against the original.

IQ Test:
Biased toward the literate.

The Three R's:
Reading, Writing and Arithmetic. (Why does only one of them begin with an R?)

Well-stocked Home Library:
Where you can find the complete works of Dickens, Chaucer, Proust, Longfellow and Shakespeare. And there are also some books for reading.

Love:
The comedy of Eros.

Lover's Leap:
The distance from one bed to another.

Taxes:
A big state with lots of cowboys.

Females:
You can't live with them and you can't do most positions without them.

Men:
Like bananas, the older they get the less firm they are.

Old Husband:
A man whose thoughts have turned from passion to pension.

Old Optimist:
A ninety year old man who marries a twenty year old woman, then looks for a home close to a school.

God:
In the beginning he made the heavens and the earth — but not much since.

Darwin:
The man who made a monkey out of God.

Male Atheist:
A man with no invisible means of support.

Holy Water:
Made by boiling the hell out of it.

Heaven, Purgatory, Hell:
The original triple threat.

Missionary Position:
Better than having no religion at all.

Murderer's Defence:
"She stabbed herself with the knife I was holding."

Considerate Murderess:
One who shoots her husband with a bow and arrow so as not to wake the children.

Confident Jury:
One that announces, "We find the defendant incredibly guilty."

Hard Time Prison:
Where the TVs are all in black and white.

Thief:
A man of conviction.

Arsehole:
A gender free concept.

An Appeal:
Asking one court to show its contempt for another court.

Ugly Arse:
One that's riddled with more pimples than an acned teenager.

Rebuttal:
An arse transplant.

Constipation:
To have and to hold.

Great Sense of Smell:
Being able to detect an ants fart from 100 yards away.

Scratching One's Arse:
Some people do it when they're thinking 'cause that's where there brain is.

Haemorrhoids:
The real grapes of wrath.

Trick Photography:
A lot of focus-pocus.

Crick:
Then noise made when you snap a picture on a Japanese camera.

Cheese:
The source of many a dazzling photographic smile.

Cartoonist:
A doodler by profession.

Sculptor:
A person who creates his work whittle by whittle.

Absent-Minded Sculptor:
Puts his model to bed and starts chiselling on his wife.

Artist:
A man who wants to paint his model in the nude, but she insists he keeps his clothes on.

Picasso Paintings:
They make you wonder what he fanaticised when he masturbated.

Extremely Abstract Painting:
One that's not painted on any canvas —you simply think about it.

Painting of a Government Department:
A still life.

Angry Artist:
Someone who loses his tempera.

Architects:
People who often suffer from an edifice complex. It's been said they cover their mistakes with ivy.

Aborted Foetus in Prague:
A cancelled Czech

Rat Coats:
Garments that are sure to put animal rights groups into conflict.

Dinosaur:
A colossal fossil who had no mazel.

Evolution:
The process by which today's wife has gone from dishpan hands to push-button fingers.

Civilisation:
The progress from shoeless toes to toeless shoes.

Family Tree:
One that can always be counted on to produce some nuts.

Killing Yourself:
A way of saying to God, "You can't fire me —I quit!"

Philosopher:
Someone who, when he goes to work, sits and thinks.

Meditation:
Better than sitting and doing nothing.

True Flatterer:
Someone who would say things to your face that they'd never say behind your back.

Real Charmer:
A person who has the ability to tell you to go to hell in such a way that you'll look forward to the trip.

Creative Writer:
Something that's great to be, but plagiarism is faster.

Sexual Encounters:
A beautiful thing between two people —and fantastic between three!

Love Triangle:
One that often results in a wrecktangle. It's an entanglement that calls for perfect timing — two-timing.

Frigid Wife:
One who has gender but not sex.

Old Maid:
A woman who, just before she dies says, "Who said you can't take it with you?"

Abstinence:
Something that isn't a bad thing if practiced in moderation.

Familiarity:
Breeds.

Natural Childbirth Class:
A great place to meet women. And you can be absolutely certain they screw.

Mick Jagger:
A man who looks like he has child-bearing lips.

Old Morality:
Crossing your legs, as opposed to the new morality which is crossing your fingers.

Artificial Insemination:
A technical knockup.

Security Guard at a Nudist Colony:
A great job, except when it comes to pinning on the badge.

What's Right:
What's left after you do everything wrong.

Suspicious:
What you become when you arrive home and find the parrot gagged.

Good News:
Never comes in an envelope with a window.

Imagination:
The thing that allows a politician to believe he's a statesman

Weather Forecast:
Something that's not always accurate. For instance, this morning I shovelled twelve inches of partly cloudy from my driveway.

Major Worry:
Thinking that these may be the good old days.

Progress:
A cannibal using a fork.

Cannibal Restaurant:
Where the food is an arm and a leg.

Wealthy Ethiopian:
A man who is able to carpet his toilet. Someday he'll be able to concrete the path to it.

Monday:
When certain restaurants close — it's the day they wash the dishes.

Old Fashioned Washing Machine:
A rock!

Great Laundry:
An establishment that gives you back your shirts all nice and white —even the blue ones.

Modern Motorways:
Roads that now make it possible for you to travel from coast to coast hardly seeing anything.

Rush Hour:
Surely a misnoma—after all it's the time of day when traffic is crawling.

Pedestrian:
A man who has two cars, a wife and a twenty year old son.

Rickshaw:
A foreign convertible.

Ford Raffle:
Second prize is a car —first prize is a parking space.

Traffic Lights:
Clever devices that safely get pedestrians halfway across the street.

Skiing:
A sport you can learn in ten easy sittings.

Steroids:
Often taken by athletes, but why chess players?

Mechanic:
An Amish guy with his arm up a horse's arse.

Tough Luck:
Failing to make the chess team because of your height.

Computer:
A machine that can usually beat a human in chess but it's no match for a person when it comes to kick boxing.

Tennis:
Basically ping-pong, except the players stand on the table.

Karate:
A sport in which you practice breaking boards so you'll be able to protect yourself the next time you're attacked by a board.

Hourglass Figure:
On some women most of the sand has gone to the bottom.

Moth Balls:
Not always easy to smell —after all, it's difficult to get their little legs apart.

Virgin Wool:
Comes from sheep that can outrun the shepherd.

Corporate Virgin:
A girl who's new to the firm.

Frisking:
A type of search. (If it wasn't for the frisking at airports some people would have no sex life at all.)

Don't/Stop:
The two four-letter words most offensive to men unless, of course, they're spoken together.

Penis:
Not all that it's cracked up to be. After all it has a head but no brains, there's always a couple of nuts following it around, it's closest neighbour is an arsehole, and its best friend is a cunt!

Puberty:
The age you beat around the bush.

Premature Ejaculation:
A man's way of saying how happy he is to see you.

Dirty Dancing:
The perpendicular expression of a horizontal desire.

Swedish Girl:
A smorgas broad.

Macho Woman:
A female who rolls her own tampons.

Speech Impediment:
An Italian with one arm missing.

Courtship:
That period during which a man and a woman decide whether or not they can do any better.

Sex:
Fuck by its generic name. It's nobody's business but the three people involved.

Group Sex:
A type of party that presents a minor problem —who do you thank?

Vagina:
The jaws of sex.

Teenage Manage a Trois:
Using both hands to masturbate.

Great Idea:
A braille edition of Playboy.

Perfect Female:
A woman whose size is 36-24-36 —and her other breast is the same.

Breast Feeding:
Living off Mother Nurture.

Illegitimate Child:
A sinfant.

Wrinkles:
 An inherited trait—you get it from your children.

Great Advice:
Have children while your parents are young enough to take care of them.

Eternal Triangle:
Nappies.

Accordion:
A bagpipe with pleats, also thought of as a stomach Steinway.

Drummers:
Musicians who use the rhythm method.

Difficult:
Playing The Flight Of The Bumblebee on a trombone in a telephone booth.

Operetta:
A woman who works for the telephone company.

Ballet Student:
Someone who improves in leaps and bounds.

True Musician:
A man who, when he hears a beautiful girl singing in the shower, puts his ear to the keyhole.

Arab:
A muslim in muslin.

Saudi Arabian Comedian:
A man who asks the audience, "Has anyone ever been convicted of stealing? Raise your hand!"

Pretend:
Something you can do to be serious, but not to be witty.

Mummies:
Egyptians who were pressed for time.

Workaholic Undertaker:
A man who buries himself in his work.

Undertakers Wife:
A woman who gets mad when her husband brings home his work.

Business Executive:
A man who talks golf at the office, and business on the golf course.

Titian:
An artist whose paintings are often imiTitians.

Booming Business:
A period when sales are so good the boss needs two secretaries—one for each knee.

Late Secretary:
It takes her an hour to get to work —and that's after she arrives.

Crying Secretary:
A woman whose just been told by the boss that she's not pretty enough to make so many mistakes.

Job Assessment Test:
For some people results show they're most suited for early retirement.

Ten Best Paid Jobs:
Begging is up to number seven.

Die:
The very last thing a person wants to do.

Widow:
A woman who always knows where her husband is at night.

Mourning Widower:
A man who insists upon black olives in his martinis.

Geriatric Martini:
Gin and vermouth with a prune.

Impotence:
Nature's way of saying, "No hard feelings."

Old Man's Fantasy:
Having two women at the same time —one to cook and one to clean.

Eastbourne:
God's waiting room.

England:
A country in which any kid could grow up to become Prime Minister —— it's just one of the chances they take.

Thailand:
A place where the farming is very advanced. Crops are always rotated —opium one year, hashish the next.

Hong Kong:
Where you can find thousands of junk souvenirs marked, MADE IN AMERICA.

UN:
A unison of nations in which there are two China's— one from Column A and one from Column B.

Pleasure Trip:
Taking your wife to the airport.

Hobby:
For some women it's the neighbour's hubby.

Schizophrenic's Convention:
Attended by anyone who is everyone.

Bad Day:
When your wife leaves you for your best friend, so on the same day you lose your wife as well as Rover.

Bigamy:
The only crime in which two rites make a wrong.

Cupid:
Although a superb shot with a bow and arrow, he's made a lot of bad Mrs.

Irish Queer:
A man who prefers women to alcohol.

Pretty Wife:
One who looks as lovely as when she was first married —only it takes a little longer now.

Economical Wife:
One who uses thirty-five candles on her fortieth birthday.

Children:
Youngsters who wonder why dad gets grayer as mum gets blonder.

Suicide Blonde:
Dyed by her own hands.

Gay Lumberjack:
His name is Spruce.

Cold Weather:
Very dangerous for women in Hollywood. At low temperatures silicone freezes.

Christmas:
A time when the bin men are suddenly saying hello.

Father Christmas:
A man who complains he's getting fed up with making house calls.

Crazy Optimist:
Someone who has just eaten the leg from a thirty-pound turkey at a Christmas dinner, and the next day asks, "What's for lunch?"

Intravenous Feeding:
The main complaint is the lack of flavour.

Marriage:
A wonderful institution —it's great to find that one special person you want to aggravate for the rest of your life.

Remarrying:
Something you do when the divorce isn't working out.

Going Bald:
A condition which a man is gradually forced to accept as the conversations with his barber get shorter and shorter.

Conscience:
The thing that feels bad when everything else feels good. It doesn't stop you from doing anything —it just keeps you from enjoying it.

Extreme Ugliness:
Something you become aware of when a proctologist puts his finger in your mouth.

Calories:
Weight lifters.

Reducing Salon:
A place that takes your breadth away.

Can't Fail Diet:
You eat whatever you want —you just don't swallow.

Chinese Diet:
On this diet you can also eat whatever you want, but you can only use one chopstick.

Jogging Backwards:
An exercise in which you gain weight.

Neat Fat Lady:
A woman who has every chin right in place.

H2 Ugh!:
The new chemical formula for water.

Milk:
Grass once removed.

Fish:
Creatures who like to take their holiday at the same time as anglers.

Unrealistic Optimist:
Someone who goes into a fish restaurant and orders oysters, hoping to pay for them with a pearl.

Lobster:
Eaten by some for taste, by others for nourishment, but by most for exercise. Have you ever noticed that the more of it you eat, the more you leave on your plate?

Dishevelled:
The opposite of shevelled.

Penthouse:
A flat with a roof under your feet.

A Fat Chance:
A strange expression —it means the same as a slim chance.

Fear of Heights:
A common fear —what's less common is the fear of widths.

True Insomniac:
A person who, even when he's sleeping, dreams he's awake.

Jewish Dropout:
Any student that didn't get a Ph.D.

Playboy:
A magazine that's taught millions of husbands to look bored while turning pages.

Dawn:
The name of a very sexy single woman. She's the reason so many men like to awake at the crack of Dawn.

Prurient Interest:
Everything is relative - to a banker it's almost 20%.

Barbershop:
Where they always have magazines devoted to poor unfortunate women - the ones who can't even afford clothes.

Campers:
People who fall into two categories - backpackers and six packers.

Yawning during an X rated film:
A guy suffering from indecent composure.

Red China:
A country with almost a billion people, and they try to claim Ping Pong is their national sport.

Make love not war:
The bumper sticker on the car of an obstetrician.

Female Lobbyist:
Everytime a convention comes to town they hang around the lobby.

Middle Age:
When you're not interested in turning the TV set off or your husband on.

Italian Men:
To a female tourist visiting Italy they're half-men, half-lobster.

Shortest history book - chapter one:
Many years ago there was a garden called Eden. In it lived two people - Adam and Bruce.

Willpower:
Going to a topless restaurant and looking at the menu.

Birth control pills:
Medication that's deductible, but only if they don't work.

Sex - Chinese style:
Everytime you get romantic with your wife she screams "Won Ton, Won Ton." That's NOT NOW , NOT NOW backwards.

Modern Females:
Take vitamin pills to put them in shape and birth control pills to keep them that way.

Male Hairdressers:
Men who hate chess - they won't have anything to do with a game in which the Queen is expendable.

Sex at the office:
At least nobody comes in to tell you how to do it faster.

Streetwalker:
A woman whose looked at more ceilings than Michaelangelo.

Antique bedwarmer:
An ninety year old prostitute.

Misery:
Your wife complaining about a shortage - and you're on honeymoon.

A female wary of men:
Try to help her on with her coat and she'll yell, "Rape."

Red light district:
Where Jehovah's witnesses knock on your door and say, "We bring you love." This is nice because in this neighbourhood single men often have to send out for it.

Titty Implants:
Today when it comes to women, men don't really know what they're up against.

Male chauvinist pig:
Men who agree with the Japanese view of women - that they're a thing of beauty and a toy forever.

Marriage:
Natures way of keeping men from fighting with strangers.

Eskimo:
A guy who keeps looking to get a nose job.

Pussy Punishment:
Beating around the bush.

Adult Movies:
It all depends where you're from. In quiet suburban villages they're known as licentious pornographic tools of the devil. In Shepperton they're known as X-rated flicks. For people who live in Soho they're known as home movies.

Film Buff:
A person who'll go to any movie if the cast is in the buff.

Major Worry:
Seeing your little son finger painting, – with nail polish!

Modern straight-laced women:
A female who says, "Stop that you. Not you, you.

Communes:
A place that's a hot bed of hot beds.

Today's Schools:
Where they teach kids what to do in bed but not how to make them.

Xstablishments:
Theatres that show porno films.

Wife-swapping club:
One with no dues, and very few don'ts.

King of the underworld:
A gynaecologist.

Eskimo Nymphomaniac:
A female with a very sore nose.

Cunnilingus:
Eating around the bush.

Real Loser:
A guy who tries to see a porno film but the cashier won't sell him a ticket - she claims she has a headache.

Modern Women:
Females who are above showing their knees to attract men - far above it.

Twiggy:
A woman who was once asked to burn her bra, but she turned them down flat.

Film Theatres:
While a movie might be rated PG what goes on in some of the seats is X.

Porno Theatre:
Where you've never seen such raw, blatant sex. And it's even worse on the screen.

Gay Marriage:
Where the mothers say to themselves, "I'm not losing a son, I'm gaining a son."

Vasectomy:
The stitch in time that saves nine.

Trouble in the garden of Eden:
First started when Eve said to Adam, "What do you mean the kids don't look like you?"

Beneficiary:
An eager bereaver.

Weight watchers motto:
TUBBY OR NOT TUBBY - that is the question.

George Washington:
A man who had a wooden set of teeth. He brushed after every meal and saw his carpenter twice a year.

Doctors:
Over the years they've learned how to better reduce the swelling - in your wallet.

Fat Farms:
Places where you go to lose weight. on the first day alone you lose at least 100 pounds.

Italian Beauty Queen:
A pizza ass.

A department store Father Christmas:
A man who suffers from water on the knee - at least three or four times a day.

Television:
A device that brings characters into your living room that you'd never have in your house.

The Vatican:
Where traffic lights say KNEEL, DON'T KNEEL.

Christmas Dinner:
At the end you have a touch of the bubbly - alka seltzer.

Beauty Contest:
Where dozens of gorgeous girls are in bathing suits and the male judges are in heaven.

Trying to eliminate poverty:
A ridiculous idea - it's all some of us have left.

Distant Relative:
Someone you've lent money to.

A Dead Bambi:
The deer departed.

Domineering Boss:
Someone who places the suggestion box on the paper shredder.

Niagara Falls:
Proof that teamwork works. After all, it's nothing but a lot of little drips working together.

Tuba:
A trumpet with a glandular problem.

Truly Obese:
When your shadow weighs 25 pounds.

Office fire alarm system:
As soon as someone is fired everyone knows about it.

Fear:
Taking your kid to a remedial maths course and the person sitting next to him is your accountant.

Sad Story:
A butcher wanted to become a brain surgeon but couldn't afford the cut in pay.

Pasta:
If there's any truth in advertising they'd call it Fattecini.

Beverly Hills:
A place that's so chic the traffic lights come in decorator colours.

Arabs:
People who have an interesting philosophy - walk softly and carry a big dipstick.

Black Ice:
The kind that allows you to get 20 miles to the gallon even when your foot is on the brake.

Impeachment:
Premature ejectulation.

Paying tax on the honour system:
"Yes your Honour, no your Honour..."

Some British Trains:
Forty – mile an hour slums.

Experienced Train Riders:
A person who never orders soup that doesn't match his pants.

Bankruptcy:
When you go from a credit rating to a credit rotting.

Auto Insurance:
So high some people have to sell their car to pay for it.

Stock Market:
Some people want to spell it with a "U instead of an O."

Country Music:
The kind that could use a little fresh air.

George Bush ski slope:
So named because it's downhill all the way.

Horse:
An animal that's never sure if it will be glue, meat, or transportation.

Goldfish with rheumatism:
The vet says the only cure is to keep them out of damp places.

Ten year olds:
The only four letter word they don't know is soap.

Gardener's Motto:
In Sod we trust.

Antiques Collector:
A junk junkie.

Busy Secretary:
One who comes to work and files continually for eight hours a day - her nails.

Death Penalty:
The only sure way to stop people from squeezing toothpaste from the middle of the tube.

Iraqi Generals:
Military men who really know how to back up their troops.

Senseless Hi-jacker:
Someone who buys a round trip ticket.

Bupa:
A form of medical insurance which has made it possible for millions of Brits to be ill at ease.

Plastic Surgeons:
Medical practitioners who prefer to work on politicians, because they never reject any graft.

Population Explosion:
When a teenager gets pregnant and it's the parents that blow up.

Ushers:
Compulsive seaters.

Religious TV Channel:
Where they use canned reverence.

Low grade infection:
What parents get when they see their kid's report card - it makes them sick.

Cure for smoking in bed:
Buy a water bed and fill it with petrol.

Smokers:
People who puff on cigarettes, cigars, pipes and stairs.

Petrol:
Now so expensive some women don't know whether to put it in the tank or behind their ears.

New York City:
The worst place for kids at Halloween. They ring the doorbell and by the time the tenant looks through the peephole, unlocks three locks, slides the bolt back, unhooks the chain, disconnects the burglar alarm and leashes the rotweiler, it's Christmas.

Heavy Traffic:
That's when you sit in a taxi for half an hour and the only thing that moves is the meter.

Travel:
The person that said, "You can't take it with you," never saw my wife pack for a trip.

Guitars:
Very popular instruments because they're so easy to learn. For instance, my son knows two chords - one of them's C and the other isn't.

Work:
Very important. If it wasn't for work where would people rest up from their holidays?

Microscope:
An instrument that let's you see the funny side of marriage.

America:
The only country in the world where people jog ten miles a day for exercise, then take elevators to the mezzanine.

Modern Films:
Movies that often have indeterminate ratings - they're halfway between PG and PU.

Goliath:
A giant who was not killed by David. Instead he spent his whole life working for slingshot control.

Muscle Man:
A guy who works out in the gym so much that even his eyebrows have biceps.

Ping Pong Paddle:
A tongue depressor for Mick Jagger.

Gas Pains:
What you get when you've just filled your tank with petrol and it's cost you fifty pounds.

Ignorance:
Is said to be bliss - so why aren't more people happy?

Rock Bands:
Musicians who bring to a gig such expensive microphones, amplifiers and instruments, you wonder how they can afford it. Then you realise how much money they've saved on music lessons.

Accurate Cricket Bowler:
One who never misses the bat.

Great Aftershave Lotion:
One that drives a woman crazy - it smells like money.

Meat:
Now so expensive that Dracula isn't the only one who can be killed by a steak.

Mothers-in-law:
Women you give a broom to then say, "Ride it in good health."

Tony Blair:
A man who tells his wife he's just signed a ten billion pound bill and his wife says, "That's nice - now take out the rubbish."

Margaret Thatcher:
A women who was once Prime Minister. Many people still feel she was the best man for the job.

Acupuncture:
An alternative therapy that no doubt works. When's the last time you saw a sick porcupine.

Tipping:
Like prunes, you always have to ask yourself, "Is one enough, is five too many?"

Don Juan Drinker:
Drink Juan and you're Don.

New Year's Sympathy Card:
For any man who at the stroke of twelve, is standing next to his wife.

New Years Day:
When government workers turn over a new loaf.

Hostile Wife:
A woman who calls her husband sugar, honey, sweetie, knowing full well he's a diabetic.

Very old used car:
It has one great advantage - you never have to change the oil every 2,000 miles - that's' because there's never any left.

Magicians:
A vanishing species.

Used Cars:
Sometimes owned by little old ladies – it's often the car that's aged them.

Advice to newly married men:
The first thing you should do is take your little black book and burn it - into your memory.

Glowworm Marriage:
To a woman it's when the glow is over but the worm remains.

Crazy Optimist:
Someone who jumps off the top of a skyscraper and as he passes the 30th floor says to himself, "Well I'm okay so far."

Good news, Bad news:
Your wife coming home to say, "18 out of 20 on my drivers test, – unfortunately they happen to be pedestrians."

The importance of women:
Remember Eve was only a side issue.

Depression:
When Joe Jones and Dow Jones have the same average.

Golf Champions:
People who think that money grows on tees.

Winning the lottery:
A relative achievement – win and you keep hearing from relatives.

A.A.:
Members make souse calls.

Overweight:
What you get when you take the butter with the sweet.

Cheap Toupee:
Don't buy it - you start losing hair that isn't even yours.

Street Crime:
Now becoming so bad that yesterday Clark Kent went into a phone booth and was afraid to come out.

Death:
Suffered by people who procrastinate - they wait to the last possible second for it to happen.

Modern Colleges:
Admit students who make straight A's, and even those who make their B's a little crooked.

Truly Dumb Kid:
A three year old who has to take remedial sandpile.

Love at first sight:
Saves a lot of time.

Prize Salesman:
The guy who was able to sell underarm deodourant to octopi.

Efficiency Expert:
Someone who loves to attend the ballet - it's the only chance he gets to see working people really on their toes.

Zimbabwe:
One of the countries in which you're in danger of getting mugged AFTER you get to the police station.

Plumber:
A guy who could get fifty pounds an hour. Just saying, "Good morning," costs you £1.50!

Realist:
A husband who hears his wife say, "I'll be ready in two minutes," so he picks up something to read - War and Peace.

Southern California:
A state that's known for its avant-God religions.

A Little:
It's a lot when it's all you've got.

True Coward:
A guy who refuses to play Russian Roulette even with a water pistol.

The Truth:
Shall make you free. Unless you're a criminal, in which case the courts will make you free.

Politicians:
People who often need a course in remedial humility.

Two Big Worries:
First, we may never get back to the good old days. Second, these may be them!

Truly Cut-rate Manicurist:
Someone who doesn't actually trim your nails with a scissor – she bites them!

The Wright Brothers:
It's said they learned how to fly by watching the birds. It's a good thing they didn't watch rabbits or we'd all be hopping.

Prune Juice:
They say if you drink enough you'll never catch cold. Of course not – you'll never have time enough to get outside to catch one!

Temptation:
Comes easy - opportunity takes a little longer.

Vitamin C Overdose:
You break out in grapefruit.

Wall Street:
Where prophets tell us what will happen and profits tell us what did happen.

Conservationists:
People who pour trouble on oiled waters.

Tolerant Children:
Kids who look upon their dad as the square in the family circle.

Dude Ranch:
A game that's engaged in by modern young children. It's not unlike playing house, with a little more horsing around.

Irish Wedding:
Instead of rice they throw potatoes.

Inflation:
That's when the tip you leave at lunch used to buy one.

American Indian Male Physique:
The kind that women take one look at and say, "Ugh."

Integrity:
That's when a man refuses to even mow the lawn because he's collecting unemployment benefits for not working.

Natural Death:
Being hit by a car.

Waist:
The place between the breast and hips. It's so-called because another pair of tits could be there.

Indifferent:
The complaint of many wives about their husbands. And with some wives the complaint is separated into two words.

Topless/Bottomless Club:
You go in and no one is there.

Aspiring Porn Actors:
Men who face a lot of STIFF competition.

Government Payroll:
With some governments it's a matter of relative importance.

Ship of State:
One vessel that often moves in a fog.

Birth:
The leading cause of death.

Lady Chatterley's Lover:
A man who was a bit rough around the hedges.

Diplomacy:
Letting someone else have your way.

Caution:
When you're scarred. (Cowardice is when the other guy is scarred).

Cynic:
One who looks down upon those above him.

School Days:
The happiest days of your life - but only if your kids are old enough to attend.

Cockiness:
The feeling you have just before you know better.

The Future:
Where you spend the rest of your life.

Cocktail Party:
Where olives are speared and acquaintances stabbed.

Termites:
Insects that take a coffee table break.

Young Priest:
A man who feels tortured having to give up his sex life, only to have people tell him the highlights of theirs.

Election Day:
When 25 million people take the day off from work to vote – and 15 million of them do.

Alimony:
The bounty on the mutiny. (A man's transition from a co-starring part to a supporting role.)

Circus Accountant:
Someone who really knows how to juggle the books.

Tact:
The ability that some people have to make their guests feel at home when they wish they were.

Conductor:
A guy who often throws tempo tantrums.

Taxes:
A big State with lots of cowboys.

Adultery:
The application of democracy to love.

Rhubarb:
Bloodshot celery.

other POWERFRESH titles

POWERFRESH TONI GOFFE TITLES

1902929411	FINISHED AT 50	2.99 ☐
1902929403	FARTING	2.99 ☐
190292942X	LIFE AFTER BABY	2.99 ☐

POWERFRESH MAD SERIES

1874125783	MAD TO BE FATHER	2.99 ☐
1874125694	MAD TO BE A MOTHER	2.99 ☐
1874125686	MAD ON FOOTBALL	2.99 ☐
187412552X	MAD TO GET MARRIED	2.99 ☐
1874125546	MAD TO HAVE A BABY	2.99 ☐
1874125619	MAD TO HAVE A PONY	2.99 ☐
1874125627	MAD TO HAVE A CAT	2.99 ☐
1874125643	MAD TO BE 40 HIM	2.99 ☐
1874125651	MAD TO BE 40 HER	2.99 ☐
187412566X	MAD TO BE 50 HIM	2.99 ☐

POWERFRESH FUNNYSIDE SERIES

1874125260	FUNNY SIDE OF 30	2.99 ☐
1874125104	FUNNY SIDE OF 40 HIM	2.99 ☐
1874125112	FUNNY SIDE OF 40 HER	2.99 ☐
190292911X	FUNNY SIDE OF 50 HIM	2.99 ☐
1874125139	FUNNY SIDE OF 50 HER	2.99 ☐
1874125252	FUNNY SIDE OF 60	2.99 ☐
1874125279	FUNNY SIDE OF SEX	2.99 ☐

POWERFRESH OTHER A5

1874125171	"CRINKLED "N" WRINKLED"	2.99 ☐
1874125376	A MOTHER NO FUN	2.99 ☐
1874125449	WE'RE GETTING MARRIED	2.99 ☐
1874125481	CAT CRAZY	2.99 ☐
190292908X	EVERYTHING MEN KNOW ABOUT SEX	2.99 ☐
1902929071	EVERYTHING MEN KNOW ABOUT WMN	2.99 ☐
1902929004	KISSING COURSE	2.99 ☐
1874125996	CONGRATULATIONS YOU'VE PASSED	2.99 ☐
1902929276	TOILET VISITORS BOOK	2.99 ☐
1902929160	BIG FAT SLEEPY CAT	2.99 ☐

POWERFRESH SILVEY JEX TITLES

1902929055	FART ATTACK	2.99 ☐
1874125961	LOVE & PASSION 4 THE ELDERLY	2.99 ☐
187412597X	A BABY BOOK	2.99 ☐
1874125996	SHEEP 'N' NASTY	2.99 ☐
1874125988	SPORT FOR THE ELDERLY	2.99 ☐
1902929144	FUN & FROLICS FOR THE ELDERLY	2.99 ☐

POWERFRESH HUMOUR

1874125945	GUIDE TO SEX & SEDUCTION	3.99 ☐
1874125848	DICK'S NAUGHTY BOOK	3.99 ☐
190292925X	MODERN BABES LB OF SPELLS	4.99 ☐
1902929268	A MUMS LB OF SPELLS	4.99 ☐

POWERFRESH LITTLE SQUARE TITLES

1902929330	LS DIRTY JOKES	2.50 ☐
1902929314	LS DRINKING JOKES	2.50 ☐
1902929322	LS GOLF JOKES	2.50 ☐
190292939X	LS IRISH JOKES	2.50 ☐
1902929292	LS TURNING 18	2.50 ☐
1902929977	LS TURNING 21	2.50 ☐
1902929969	LS THE BIG 30	2.50 ☐
1902929241	LS THE BIG 40	2.50 ☐
1902929233	LS THE BIG 50	2.50 ☐
1902929284	LS BIG 60	2.50 ☐
1902929225	LS SINGLE V MARRIED WOMEN	2.50 ☐

1902929217	LS YES BUT...!	2.50 ☐
1902929306	LS WHISKY	2.50 ☐
1902929500	LS HOW TO PULL BY MAGIC	2.50 ☐

POWERFRESH STATIONARY TITLES

1902929381	WEDDING GUEST BOOK	9.99 ☐
1902929349	WEEKLY PLANNER CATS	6.99 ☐
1902929357	WEEKLY PLANNER DOGS	6.99 ☐
1902929365	WEEKLY PLANNER COTTAGES	6.99 ☐
1902929373	WEEKLY PLANNER OFFICE	6.99 ☐
1902929519	HUMDINGER TELEPHONE BOOK	4.99 ☐
1902929527	HUMDINGER ADDRESS BOOK	4.99 ☐
1902929535	HUMDINGER NOTEBOOK	2.99 ☐

Name

Address

P&P £1.00 Per Parcel

Please send cheques payable to Powerfresh LTD

To Powerfresh LTD 21 Rothersthorpe Crescent

Northampton NN4 8JD